Acknowledgements

Learning to risk again appeared in *To Risk Again*, Bookman Publishing & Marketing, 2008.

He was goat-footed appeared in *Shaking Up the Insides of the Word*, Mellon Poetry Press, New York, 1992.

The Dreamer And The Poet appeared in *Shaking Up the Insides of the Word*, Mellon Poetry Press, New York, 1992.

Even a mt. poet should be able to write something appeared in *Appalachian Journal*, Volume 12 Number 3, Spring 1985.

Poem in the Afternoon, appeared in the anthology, *The New Poetry In Love*, Nicky Jones, editor, 2008, United Kingdom.

Doubt appeared in *Pegasus*, 1976.

Into the Room Where Poetry Lies appeared in *Appalachian Heritage*.

Writing a novel appeared in *miller's pond*, Vol. 9, Issue 1, 2006.

The front cover is of Anna Akhmatova, a portrait done in black crayon from the Paul Alexandre collection. Modigliani portrays Anna as an ancient Egyptian goddess. He also captures the look of the poet lost in a dream. It is a rare erotic drawing of Anna.

Table of Contents

Chapter One	page 7
Chapter Two	page 8
Chapter Three	page 10
Chapter Four	page 11
Chapter Five	page 12
Chapter Six	page 13
Chapter Seven	page 14
Chapter Eight	page 15
Chapter Nine	page 17
Chapter Ten	page 18
Chapter Eleven	page 19
Chapter Twelve	page 20
Chapter Thirteen	page 21
Chapter Fourteen	page 22
Chapter Fifteen	page 23
Chapter Sixteen	page 24
Chapter Seventeen	page 25
Chapter Eighteen	page 26
Chapter Nineteen	page 27
Chapter Twenty	page 28
Chapter Twenty-One	page 30
Chapter Twenty-Two	page 31
Chapter Twenty-Three	page 32
Chapter Twenty-Four	page 33
Chapter Twenty-Five	page 35
Chapter Twenty-Six	page 36
Chapter Twenty-Seven	page 37
Chapter Twenty-Eight	page 38
Chapter Twenty-Nine	page 39
Chapter Thirty	page 41
Chapter Thirty-One	page 43
Chapter Thirty-Two	page 45
Chapter Thirty-Three	page 46

Poems are dangerous necessities

A Poetry Novel

2011

Rudy Thomas

OLD SEVENTY CREEK PRESS POETRY SERIES 2011

In silence the heart raves. It utters words meaningless, that never had a meaning. I was ten, skinny, red-headed, freckled, in a big black Buick, driven by a big grown boy, with a necktie. She sat in front of the drugstore, sipping something through a straw. There is nothing like Beauty. It stops your heart. It thickens your blood. It stops your breath. It makes you feel dirty. You need a hot bath. I leaned against a telephone pole, and watched. I thought I would die if she saw me.

Excerpt set to prose
from the poem:
True Love by Robert Penn Warren

From: **Poem without a Hero**

Paris is in dark mist
And probably again Modigliani
Imperceptibly follows me.
He has a sad virtue
To bring disorder even to my dreams
And be the reason of my many misfortunes.

Anna Akhmatov

Chapter Thirty-Four	page 48
Chapter Thirty-Five	page 50
Chapter Thirty-Six	page 51
Chapter Thirty-Seven	page 52
Chapter Thirty-Eight	page 53
Chapter Thirty-Nine	page 54
Chapter Forty	page 56
Chapter Forty-One	page 57
Chapter Forty-Two	page 58
Chapter Forty-Three	page 59
Chapter Forty-Four	page 61
Chapter Forty-Five	page 63
Chapter Forty-Six	page 64
Chapter Forty-Seven	page 65
Chapter Forty-Eight	page 66
Chapter Forty-Nine	page 68
Chapter Fifty	page 70
Chapter Fifty-One	page 71
Chapter Fifty-Two	page 72
Chapter Fifty-Three	page 73
Chapter Fifty-Four	page 74
Chapter Fifty-Five	page 75
Chapter Fifty-Six	page 76
Chapter Fifty-Seven	page 77
Chapter Fifty-Eight	page 78
Chapter Fifty-Nine	page 79
Chapter Sixty	page 80
Chapter Sixty-One	page 81
Chapter Sixty-Two	page 82
Chapter Sixty-Three	page 83
Chapter Sixty-Four	page 84
Chapter Sixty-Five	page 86
Chapter Sixty-Six	page 87
Chapter Sixty-Seven	page 88
Chapter Sixty-Eight	page 89

Chapter Sixty-Nine	page 90
Chapter Seventy	page 91
Chapter Seventy-One	page 92
Chapter Seventy-Two	page 93
Chapter Seventy-Three	page 94
Chapter Seventy-Four	page 95
Chapter Seventy-Five	page 105
Chapter Seventy-Six	page 106

COPYRIGHT 2011 BY RUDY THOMAS

2011 OLD SEVENTY CREEK FIRST EDITION
PRINTED IN THE UNITED STATES OF AMERICA
ALL RIGHTS RESERVED UNDER INTERNATIONAL AND PAN-AMERICAN COPYRIGHT CONVENTIONS.
NO PART OF THIS WORK MAY BE USED WITHOUT WRITTEN PERMISSION FROM THE AUTHOR EXCEPT FOR LIMITED QUOTES IN A LITERARY REVIEW.
PUBLISHED IN THE UNITED STATES BY OLD SEVENTY CREEK PRESS
RUDY THOMAS, PUBLISHER
P. O. BOX 204
ALBANY, KENTUCKY 42602

ISBN: 978-0615538969
EAN: 0615538967

Chapter 1

The novel begins with a woman
on a bed in dim light,
a woman,
naked
except for shadows.
The pair becoming engrossed in each other
is the story.

The artist beside her
looks at her
& says:
Even in this dark place
your face,
your body,
your eyes
are beautiful.

The pages are blank
after he speaks.
No words describe
what the lovers do
or how long they are
together.

When the chapter ends,
Anna says to the man:
That happens very rarely with painters.

Chapter Two

The man is alone.
He dreams about the woman, Anna.
Do you want to come see me? the woman asks.

Do you mean it? he answers.

Sure, the woman says. *Hurry*...

He rushes to her even tho he dreams.
Come in, the woman says when he knocks.
He takes off his shoes at the door.
They hug, move, stop & embrace more.
You didn't have to take them off, she says.
I take off all my clothes at home, he says.

Later, the woman asks:
*If I ask you, will you
rub my shoulder?*
He continues to hold her.
I will, he answers.

On her bed, he says:
You must take these off...
She does.
& this...
She does.
He puts oil in his hand,

blows on it, for it is cool.
Do you want the window closed? He asks.
It's okay, she says.
He begins to massage her shoulder,
her neck, her toes, then her hips.

She moves her hips up & down
against him.
He leans forward on his elbows.
You best not do that, he whispers.
She moves her hips again,

then there is a blank canvas,
for the artist to paint
upon

& a blank page for her to write on.
*If I ask you to stay all night,
I think you'd say yes...*"

Yes, Modigliani says...

& there are more blank pages in the novel
before the chapter ends—
before the next canvas begins...

Chapter Three

Reading Hemingway's Poetry

Reading Hemingway's poetry, I understand
something I knew already,
but had forgotten.
His friends were better than his young words.
Yet, his words appeared on pages poets envy.

Hemingway's words improved, not as poetry,
but as prose, fiction about life, raucous when
imbibed, one true sentence, then words
that go on from there to find their place.

Reading Hemingway's poetry, I understand
something we
had forgotten:
Old Seventy Creek flows like his words,
& you & I are only

water-rounded stones, seen from above,
stained brown & we,
professing love,
refuse to surface.

Chapter Four

When you return

I will not ask you why
you went away.
I will not ask you where
you were.

Mistakes I have made;
things I have done
in my life make pale
your journey.

I will read your eyes
like I read Old Seventy Creek,
its ebb & flow
& I will know your undercurrent

& I will know everything
of love I want to know,
for I understand how the creek speaks:
an April roar, muddy outside its banks,

a trickle down
from standing pools
in August
drought.

Chapter Five

When you do not return
before April brings yellow daffodils,
I begin to think that in my mind
I will have to begin to call you
a woman again
& me the lonely poet.

When it seems there is no lovers' burn
of us within your heart, your absence fills
mine with loneliness of the worst kind,
a desert landscape. *You*
I say *are but rain to come.*
I will endure this drought, my pain.

A white ibis lands by the creek
& waits, one leg drawn up...

Chapter Six

Soliloquy of the white ibis

*Here I stand in water,
listening to the voice
of this creek.*

*I see my shadow.
I am greater than my shadow.
The sky is greater than its reflection.*

*The five sticks ahead,
greater than their slant,
but my voice cannot tell me why...*

*I know love.
It is no mistake.
I'm standing here by this water,*

*awaiting my mate.
When she arrives,
I will be vigilant.*

*I will watch for man
while she eats fry
then she will keep an eye*

*out
so I can
feast.*

Chapter Seven

To feel you

Modigliani sits alone in a cool, dark room:
Words elude me, Anna.
I close my eyes & your face,
framed by your hair as tho
you have only just emerged
from the bath,
is all I see.

I open my eyes.
To feel you,
I go back in time.
The room we are in
is dark.
Your skin is soft.
Your voice is a whisper.

Your hips move up & down...

Chapter Eight

Tennessee Waitress

I have seen them in Brazil,
in Germany, France, Italy, Greece.
I have left tips for them in Amsterdam,
London, Tijuana, Montreal.
Some flirt, tease, & talk trash
others smile or utter terms of endearment.

In Tennessee, a waitress came to my table.
She looked at me, she blushed.
Every word she spoke,
she looked at me & blushed.
Two women at the pool table,
playing to display themselves
were confident,
sure of where men's eyes focused.

When she brought the check,
I asked her: *Do you know
what makes you better than those two
women at the pool table?*

No... What? she asked.

*You can blush I told her.
Do you know who Ernest Hemingway was?*

Yes she said.

Hemingway wrote: **A woman who can't blush is worthless.**

Did I blush? she asked.

Every time you spoke to me I said.

If Hemingway wrote that, she said
I must be worth more than I ever thought.

She reminded me of a waitress
at the Hotel Modigliani in Rome
who brought me a drink from the bar
after I spent a day exploring Rome.
I sipped it in the Garden
& tipped her generously
exactly like I did that Tennessee waitress.

Chapter Nine

Writing Poetry

At first he did not tell Akhmatova
he was writing poetry
when they were apart.

He wrote instead:
I am captivated by your beauty.
You are obsessively such a part

of my being,
when I am alone,
I have to draw your true

essence; I have begun to see
it in a block of stone,
always the aesthetic ideal

& he signed off with:
Only you
could make that happen.

Chapter Ten

Learning to Draw

I always told people:
I wish I could draw,
& some of them would say:
then do it.

I can't draw a straight line
I always answered.
But I am drawing
these days.

It took Modigliani's words
spoken to Akhmatova
in a comment on the Venus de Milo
to change my mind.

He said: *women with beautiful figures*
who are worth modelling or drawing
always seem unshapely
when clothed.

These days,
I draw nudes.
Straight lines are neither necessary
nor desirable.

Chapter Eleven

In Dreams,
I have a way of falling in love
with women who love women.
A man who has never
tried to love them
may have difficulty
understanding my words.

They keep turning up in my words,
& my poetry,
with all its romance.
owes much to them.
I am a product of happenstance.
I write far

more words to them,
for them than I could have thought.
We are connected. I succumb to their songs
like ancient seafarers would.
Words, like women, ought
to have more rights than wrongs

about them.
Within my dreams,
they are sensual;
some even consensual.
In rhyme.
they are a flat surface covered
with words like colors arranged

on a Modigliani canvas.

Chapter Twelve

Modigliani Whispers into the Night

The only silence is your voice.
A neighbor's dogs bark.
Frogs croak the length of the creek.
The Nightingale has yet to arrive.

The silence of your voice;
those poets of the dark;
me writing words that reek
with you, how alive

your memory is against this chill.

Chapter Thirteen

Watching the storm

It comes,
heat lightning crossing cloud
to cloud
until the silence
gets burned thru.

Down,
down,
thunder,
thunder,
wind
drives hail
across the highway
but not your memory.

Even during the rain,
its torrent ponding
in the bottom,
I find dry,
red Kentucky clay
beneath the pine trees
& much room for you beside me,

sheltered close, cocooned,
oblivious to the world,
we might as well be Modigliani and Akhmatova
in Paris, beneath his battered, black umbrella,
quoting poetry to the beating of the rain.

Chapter Fourteen

Thoreau

comes to mind
when memories of you pass,
after I look into your eyes gazing back at
mine, as alive as Walden's pond early
in spring must have been.

His words call out & find
me & gather my feelings into one mass:
The question is not what you look at,
but what you see.
Perhaps I see more than other men

have. I see you as you
see yourself--stronger than your voice
& the curves of your body
would have men believe.
I see you as words I should gather.

Poetry has room for you
the way the world had for Thoreau's choice
of woods wherein individuality
& perpetual youth dwelt. I retrieve
a memory of your passing glance. Elated rather,

am I.

Chapter Fifteen

There is a moon

There is a moon tonight & stars
no one can ever count.
There appears to be no space between

them. I went into the hills one winter
& sat atop Jack's Knob alone-no light
around me except the stars
few & far between

clouds. It was as tho
a poem waited in Upchurch Hollow
for me to look down on it

& gather words the way
my grandmother gathered eggs up
from hidden nests in tall sedge

in time of bloom & blossom.
I looked down on it as tho
it were a Modigliani work of art.

A north wind blew snow up
to melt against my cheeks.

Chapter Sixteen

I hear my voice

in this place where I sit
in morning shadows beneath a cliff.
It whispers words the way the wind whispers.
It is joyful, leaping like the water
of Old Seventy Creek over the falls.
It sings, a finch in Chestnut Oak above me.
My voice is a poem.
No one hears the silence of it.
One day, perhaps in summer,
I will write the words
into an image
of blue Forget-Me-Nots
in bloom.

Chapter Seventeen

Digging beneath a rock shelter

When I was young, the man who owned the farm
would work me & his grandson—& most times
my brother—in the hayfield above the shelter,
but he seldom let me dig for artifacts.

If I could dig, he sat, waiting to give alarm:
Time's up, young man—no mechanical chimes—
relying on his internal clock--never off-kilter,
& that would be the end of our limited contracts.

He would roll a cigarette with Prince Albert
tobacco & smoke, enjoying it, his eyes closed
as tho in prayer, never offering me one;
I would dig fast, furious, & find worked flint.

Digging beneath the rock shelter, I pull a chert
blade from the pit wall. I am no longer opposed.
I find no more joy in the silence than the sun
does in setting nor the dead farmer's squint

would have betrayed
could he have seen the thing.

Chapter Eighteen

Email from a young reader

You are my favorite poet. That's all.
I smile when I read the short of it.

& you are my favorite reader
I email to her.

*Aw, shucks, you say that to all
the 20 something year old women*

she sends back
with a smiley face.

& it is spring
& I fancy words

feel a Hemingway urge
a Modigliani moment

rush thru me.
I can't email such things

to her,
however.

Chapter Nineteen

Stopping to View

the sky,
I feel the pressure falling.
A storm will come thru
on its journey northeast. Ten daffodils,
their trumpets raised,
will be its first victims.

It is spring again.
I am no nearer a poem
than I am to your love.
The wind lashes the locust
& the wren
on the trellis...

How it sings!
Its voice knows intimacy
& trouble in the air.
I listen to each note.
The wind rises.
It flies up--away.

In the ceaseless pour of rain,
I stand until I shiver.
Inside,
later,
I cannot resist
writing the wren's words:

I am a stranger,
may my song send you
on your own journey.

Chapter Twenty

I still want to stand inside

the memory of my room,
the only space I believed you
could not take away.

I still want to stand inside

the memory of my room
& turn back the sheets
on the bed while you shower.

Instead, I must stand outside

the memory of your room,
a face placed against your window
as sunlight fades.

I want to write a poem

inside the memory of your room
& place the words, thin as a thong,
upon lines that risk

& leap & move
like the wake on Lake Cumberland
during summer.

Outside the memory of your room,
my voice sounds like
the strangest renegade voice,

the dawn throat-whistle
of a plain colored
thrush, its underbelly

spots revealed in flight.
My love for you moves
a hint of a wind,

that shakes maple's leaves
so slowly they appeared
not to move at all.

You took another

into your room
before I had time
to fall out of love.

One moment
you were lips
that brush mine.

The next,
you became this
emptiness in my chest.

Chapter Twenty-One

In just a time of ice

I came
out of my
self
& this matter called brain
waved at me

& I saw
snow thru a wall of glass
that you cannot see
for it melts

runs down
the hillside
into a creek
with no name

the clear water sinks
suddenly
emerges
far off

& becomes
Old Seventy Creek
but
you won't be able

to get there
from where you are.

Chapter Twenty-Two

Robins on the lawn

I hear them singing as dawn
creeps up Jack's Knob suddenly
& follows the sky
along banks that comfort snow,
then wades knee-deep water
against the prevailing wind toil-
ing along Old Seventy Creek.

I hear Emily Dickinson yawn,
rise up quietly
from a poem & question why
they show
up one day later
this spring, for warm soil
pulled new trumpet daffodils

up the week before.

Chapter Twenty-Three

Writing words

I space them across the page again
like paint upon white

canvas--like the footbridge
over Old Seventy Creek,

or Sewell Mountain
against evening sky

in the distance.

By happenstance,
if I pass you by

as I trek this rough terrain
know only this: I seek

poetry on each high ridge
& I long for one quick sight-

ing of you. Then
I will write my words

into a leaning tree
& leave it propped

against your heart.

Chapter Twenty-Four

The white space

The white space
of my folded page
needs words,

but do I write the song
of a quail here
or the rustle of oak leaves

on Jack's Knob in late November
or the excited opening bark
of a black-and-tan hound

beneath Sewell Bluff
or do I word the fear
that sound puts into an acorn-

fat raccoon?

The white space
of my folded page
is large enough

to hold all sounds
& all of Williams Creek
from its mountain springs

to the last falls
before it gets lost
in the blue green headwaters

of Lake Cumberland.

The white space
of my folded page
is where I could write

the words of a love song
that resonates in my memory
as one true line.

My inner voice
cannot sing
as my father could sing,

from the time I was young
until he died,
his voice kept alive

by a feeding tube
when his feet no longer
could tap rhythm

to the music
or dance to notes
up & down the scale.

I will leave
the white space
of my folded page

empty of words,
awaiting your return.

Chapter Twenty-Five

The last poem I dreamed

woke me past midnight.
There were words in it,
but they were not mine.

There was a voice,
but it was not mine
& a woman with your eyes

but no face carried two buckets
yoked on her shoulders.
She labored, climbing Jack's Knob.

I could not wake
while the woman cried & her tears
fell into different buckets.

I heard her pain
move out from her
tho she had no lips.

She did not know the mountain.
She walked it,
smelled & tasted it.

My words
could take her safely tho
to that place it was she had to go.

Chapter Twenty-Six

Of September 1
in his journal,
the monk, Thomas Merton,
wrote words,
confessing his desire
to be a saint.

He was of the mind
that he would only
get to sainthood
by writing books
at the Abbey of Gethsemani.

One July 17,
I become like the monk,
a man,
confessing his desire
for a woman
in silent meditation.

I am of the mind
that I can never
get to sainthood
by writing poetry
beside Old Seventy Creek.

I look toward the west
as I sit alone.
Given the humidity,
the heat, the dark clouds moving,
there will be rain

Chapter Twenty-Seven

The rain sings

in drop after drop
against my face,
upon my shoulders,
until I am wet.

There is something
familiar in its sound
like some voice in a poem,
like my father's when he sang.

I close my eyes
& walk thru the shower
into a torrent,
a drum roll on a green, tin roof.

My ear captures the song of a rain crow.
Along Green River, it calls,
flying, oblivious to the storm,
along muddy tail waters.

For one moment,
I imagine it to be
Modigliani's tormented voice
crying out for Anna.

Chapter Twenty-Eight

In silence
in a dark room
after the clock chimes,
I hear your laughter
as tho it were an echo
inside my soul
& I feel desire swell
the way Old Seventy creek will
after heavy rain.

In silence,
my thoughts clash against the room
hiding images & rhymes
until I am forced to sort feeling after
feeling that surges thru me. I know
less than I feel. My soul
is as boundless as silence, a well
dug deep, walled round with words. How will,
how should, how can I fill the void, the pain

of you leaving me this room of silence?

Twenty-Nine

This morning
on the sloping field
I stand in fescue
my Levi's wet past my knees
& the sun is yet asleep
beyond Jack's Knob
& the moon is awake
moving west
toward Cumberland River

This morning

I wish to twirl a muse--give her
no time to think which words best
describe her after we have survived the wake
of the night's storm. There is much of a job
to be done to clear the field--to keep
it alive & free it of the debris of trees--
to rescue
the land from worse storms gathering. The
sloping field

this morning

cannot consider a woman's insatiable lust
nor my powerful insistence.
Heavy seeded fescue gives me reason to exist.
My love for words keeps me singing
like the gray bird in the oak
whose music mocks my heart.
When the morning light comes up,
I will borrow silence from the glow.

This morning

my feelings go
more & more to take up
the pondering of thick healings. I start
to yearn for the warmth oak
fires radiate in winter, the lingering
touch of a woman's lips. I exist.
I remind myself there will be a cognizance

& a time for loving a woman
beyond any moment.

Chapter Thirty

Anna, I talked to a young man

*about those things he wished
for me to say
& he sat spellbound
drinking beer
while I tried to kill
the pain of life past
by smoking the hashish
of living present*

*& he said she would
understand
why he was late
& I told him
that women
are hormonal
& men cannot speak
such language
ever*

*& I told him
how in the wild
an elephant
can uproot a tree
& carry it
but when conditioned
as a calf to unjustly
feel
that the chain
strapped to its leg
is anchored
into the weight*

*of the earth
it will not strain
to pull its
adult leg free*

*& he asked me no
more about women
tho I told him
how unhappy I am
knowing that love
is being crazy
in the lust of first
passion
while all the world
talks of peace*

*& pursues
revolution.*

Chapter Thirty-One

Anna, I will choose a place to sculpt
& go there to chisel words
charged with feelings
& I shall put away
all my doubts
in that moment
of creation...

That is:
if reducing stone can be the creation
of anything
& I shall pick a small house
or apartment
in the center of a city
where I will be lost
by choice--
unable to speak the language--
& I shall fall in love again
with a woman who sleeps

in a room near me
on her stomach.
I will knock on her door
and knead gold words
upon her warm skin
& she will not encourage
nor resist my fingers
as they write or paint.

Tho it is early morning,
she will understand that
every word I write
generates new poems;

*every piece of stone
reveals a shapely woman.
My method is simply
to wake before she does
& watch her eyes flutter
like wildflowers moved in a breeze.*

*She may feel
the remoteness of my body
in the grainy light
of her bedroom
& know my dreams hold her
where she has been held before
tho not by me
& she will feel secure*

*but should the silent,
amorous words
that I pen
upon her fascinating figure
do nothing then I will be no more
visible than the population
of Madagascar
& my silent voice
will spin kisses unfelt
upon her parted lips*

*& there will only be
the sound
of her breath
taken in for a moment*

then let go.

Chapter Thirty-Two

Untitled

You are
like that sometimes
since you left:
untitled.

Remember, I am
the man
who asked:
Do you liked frozen grapes

& you are the woman
who asked
*Have you eaten them in the dark
from a woman's perspective?*

& I replied
I would...

Chapter Thirty-Three

Gathering wild flowers

At first I thought it to be
the beauty of those wild flowers
on the slope
that reminded me
of your face

It was a morning
of gray
shrouded light--
me walking thru
grass rain-wet.

I told myself
it was longing,
perhaps,
& nothing more
that I should credit

for such
an impromptu
flash
upon the blooms
I gathered.

I began
to read the flowers
silently
for their poetry--
the red ones

the magenta
the yellow ones
the white & yellow
daisy-rayed ones
the clustered primrose few

the goldenrods
on stems like wands
& lo
something more immediate
felt like you.

Soft it was
like your skin
against my mine--
a butterfly upon my collar
its wings up folded.

Chapter Thirty-Four

Learning to risk again

It was the last time
that I talked with Jim Wayne Miller
lamenting the fact that my words
had gone dry
like a stream
wet weather fed
that flows from mountains
disappears in drought

Learning to risk again
he said
will be like unlearning
how to fish
or be Appalachian
be the Brier
whose words
no one wants to read

Look at these dark smudges
under these eyes
he said
I risk already
the first night
in my grave
without my old
Methodist aunt
to pray for me

*I can't recall
when last I was so alone
with me*
he said
*so I will risk this much

when I die
I will leave you
my house of words
& always some new ground
to cultivate.*

Chapter Thirty-Five

In a City

In a city that has gotten too big,
where windows meet
& rain hides the sun,
you live
but your beauty
precedes you
& you will have chocolate you should not eat
to breathe your warm breath
upon & frozen grapes I will feed you
& the air I imagine will be like
laundered sheets
& I shall wish to sleep in your bed
or make love.

I know you have no paintings
on the wall above your bed
with you the model
for each canvas
but no one will recognize that
except me
& I will have you wish for woodland walks
& pillow talk so I might read poetry
to your eyes
where tiny terrors dwell
& like wild geese I will release my words
to fly in a V & you will rise to dance
beyond the circumstances
that bind you in that place & far off a lonesome
cry of a dove will be my poem.

Chapter Thirty-Six

I should have looked out the window,

Anna, earlier on this dark night
for in the moving of the maple leaves
I sense emotions gathering to flow
& I know where such feelings will take me

I should have looked out the window

& up sooner into the blackness of this night
at light that flickers between the leaves
the glow--
perhaps of some burned out star--is only

a glow
& all my eyes can never see
I know
as you.

Chapter Thirty-Seven

What was your day like

was it sun rising on fescue
waving in the wind
weaving into itself
seeds bowing each slender shaft

was it sun rising on sidewalks
a flag waving in the wind
whipping into itself
atop a tall silver pole

was it the red of Crimson clover
passion's signal to honey bees
nectar is flowing sweet
& of no risk to the taker

was it the red of a traffic light
a signal stopping the flow
of traffic way to way & a crossing
between two white lines with no risk at all

what was your day like I wonder
in one moment when I am weakened
by thoughts of you
while the sun devours darkness

Chapter Thirty-Eight

Poems are dangerous necessities

They never burn
without consuming
the soul
of the poet.

Poems are words,
naked women captured
by Modigliani on a canvas
without eyes.

If I had only
one poem to live,
I would make love to you in it
& forget about understanding passion

& tell wild turkeys
that I have planted
grain in the back field
where they may eat hidden

from a hunter's passing truck
come winter. Convinced you will
never return, I must write myself into fog
upon a page & let the sun have its way.

Chapter Thirty-Nine

When remembering comes,

there is a rush
a longing
a kind of questioning

what is it like
actually this memory
& should I

attempt to capture
something of it
for a moment longer

than a dream is long

perchance
the memory
of the leaky boat

when my father
takes me fishing
me bailing

until my arm aches
& him fishing
sculling with his left hand

casting with his right
until he hooks a largemouth
in shallow water

& I watch him fight it
watch it come up
& out of the water

one time dancing
the next
flopping backward

& all the time
the boat leaking
going down slowly

to a point then sinking
quickly to shallow bottom
& my father & I

come up laughing
& the big fish
never makes the willows

before my father
turns him about
to meet the net.

Chapter Forty

In the loft

The rocker
leans

balanced
yet

so far
off center

that I
find

myself
remembering

a time I walked a log
across Old Seventy creek

taking slow steps,
& so afraid to breathe

Chapter Forty-One

Waking to rain

I wake
the tin roof
echoes an excited rhythm

I hear
no thunder
rolling

I rise
alone & sing
its beat

a song of longing
and a song
of love

the falling rain
sings back
to my soul

sings of you
your memory
returns

but only stays with me
until there breaks
the sun.

Chapter Forty-Two

As the house creaked

Modigliani wrote: *cooling down*
from the outside in

the moon hides
behind the promise of rain

all is dark
outside the windows.

I should find
my way thru the dark

of this house
to my bed

but the words
I want to write

are asleep
with you

so far away
I cannot wake them.

Chapter Forty-Three

I went to the top

of the hill
in Athens

touched the olive
tree

among the rocks
& knowledgeable of

the illusion
that the lines

of the Parthenon
are

completely
straight

I stood
in awed

reckoning
within

without
& far from there

I write
words

with no
sense of restraint

those words
how they long

to wrestle
you into my poem

write you as a Spartan woman
with your *peplos*

dropped
in a pile

upon the arena
floor.

Chapter Forty-Four

I find myself

wanting to flee
the responsibility
I have
for being me

& take time
to find refuge
in a place
more exotic:

Santorini
with its windmills
& azure sea
that hugs its shores

or Rio
the long stretch
of volleyball nets
& thongs

of little
less
between
eye & skin

if I could have my choice
I might choose to hide
like a quilt
in plain sight,

drawn tight
about you
upon your bed
to warm your cool skin

I would choose
to be hand quilted
with lots of stitches
& many bright squares

held together
like words
upon
a page.

Chapter Forty-Five

I painted my friend

& neighbor, Pablo Picasso, today,
Modigliani told Diego Rivera,
Constantin Brancusi, the Romanian sculptor,
and the poets, Apollinair and Max Jacob
over drinks.
Then, he smoked hashish.

I have painted you already, Riv.
I want to paint Juan Gris next,
then you guys,
he pointed at the other three.

Bad behavior is as romantic as hell,
he said, then stripped naked
& walked out the door.

Chapter Forty-Six

From the Poet to the Word

I imagine that you are woman--
warm--but only in the mood
to curl around an image. You turn
your back toward me,
before you fall asleep.

I imagine that I am that man
blessed of all poets for you sleep nude
& my desires burn
hot, intimate. When you touch me,
I realize Poetry & Art will keep.

Chapter Forty-Seven

He was goat-footed

    for Modigliani

He was goat-footed, the Greek symbol of spring,
& he could play, one believes, the latest rage
for each tender young thing.
People heard in his presence reeded music,
difficult to describe.
But for those who looked upon his face,
he was not goat-footed.
He took no pleasure
in purposely holding off love.
It would ruin everything.
He would stare into a pair of lonely eyes
then plunge headlong into the embrace.

More about love,
& the memory of it,
he carved into stone.

Chapter Forty-Eight

For the woman to my left on the sidewalk in Washington, D. C.

The woman to my left looked at me.
My glance became a searching look in return.
Tho she was not immediately
as familiar as the Low Gap
on Grider's Mountain,
there was recognition on my part.

It is you, poet, she said.
*Remember, we rode together
in that stretch limo from the Detroit airport.
We sat facing each other,
you riding backward.
Remember, I had all that luggage.*

It is you, I said, thinking *we all have baggage...*

*Don't think this dress
is the only one I own,* she said.

It should be, I answered, slipping Freudian.

You are so kind to say that, she said.
May I ask you something?

Certainly, I replied.

Is it the color? she asked, pointing.
Or is it the length of this slit?

Yes it is, I answered.

The light changed.
We crossed the street.
She faded into the traffic,
moving left along the sidewalk.
I hurried toward the right,
already late for my meeting.

Chapter Forty-Nine

The Attraction

There is yet
an attraction,
a thrill
that adrenalines
my soul
when I write
& the mysterious word
breathes.

The attraction intensifies
& feeling rises to the heights
of a touch
& the flesh tingles
as tho lips have found form
in a roaming,
downward
spiral,
seeking the insides
of that word.

From the soul,
poetry flows like Old Seventy
creek toward the Falls,
gaining momentum
in a rain-fed rush
to pool like Lake Cumberland
upon the page.

Along the course,
birds sing,
minnows go with the current,
& leaves tremble in the wind
no more noticed
than the good warmth
of eyes meeting.

Chapter Fifty

The Word Became Woman

The poet touched the word
with a lover's knowing
& the reaction was
a catching of breath--quick--
at a time somewhere
between waking & sleep.

The poet touched the word
again as dawn's light, showing
thru the window, was
driving fast the thick
dewdrops from meadows where
timothy & red clover root deep.

& in that moment the word
became woman, glowing,
& the poet a man was
drawing up desire as thru a wick
that he might dare
give light to those dreams she keeps.

Chapter Fifty-One

Anna wrote to Modigliani

I shall never forget you.
I shall never forget
that golden gleam in your eyes.

I don't know how you lived
in the Impasse Falguière, Modi.
Such dire poverty...

I remember you being so poor;
we sat on a bench
in the Impasse Falguière;

you had no money for chairs,
remember; we would have had
to pay for them.

You never complained about the poverty.
I cherish the sixteen drawing you gave me.
My friends call them scandalous nudes.

I refuse to put them on my walls.
I still keep you and what we were hidden
from Nikolai tho he has a poet's eye.

Chapter Fifty-Two

Snow Falls

Snow Falls
flake after flake
now a flurry
then a blizzard...

Snow falls
likes words
upon the page,
a white landscape.

It is January in my dream
& snow falls
for the third day
in a row.

I write.
Snow falls.
No tracks
dot the landscape.

Below
where the field dips
the word hides,
waiting to rise up

& hit me
cold on the neck
with a flurry of poetry
disguised as snowballs.

Chapter Fifty-Three

Writer's Block

Where is the joy,
committed to memory
to be recalled—

memory
of you,
the word

&
a bath
in the morning

after wine
before the art
in our relationship

had passed
& the same sun
continued to rise—

oh, where
has gone the joy
of dancing naked

upon the page?

Chapter Fifty-Four

where are you, word

are you with that other poet
(the philandering one) & does he
get to watch you age
fascinated like a child
looking out the east window
upon a golden sunrise

or are you alone now
(adorned in undress)
privately seeking poetics
& might I
if you are,
entice you
with my same old line

again?

Chapter Fifty-Five

The Dreamer And The Poet

The dreamer goes to bed
with the leading lady,
slays the dragon,
& finds answers to life's
mysteries
in fantasy.

The poet shakes up
the insides
of the word.

Chapter Fifty-Six

I have not written

one poem for you.
Surely,
I wish I had
one left
to write.

When you left,
I lost
far,
far more
than I can write.

I caught
a wind-borne seed
& planted it
to grow poetry.
Forgive me my indifference.

I know well
the curve of your form
where my lips pursed
at night
& all that never

can be recalled
I know
for I have worded
those things
upon a naked line

within my soul.

Chapter Fifty-Seven

My Muse lives in fantasy

Never mind the fact that she is a muse--
she lives in fantasy,
ever searching for a poet who will give her
what she seeks.

Being a muse evokes the reality
that there is no more difficult work
than drawing words
from the deepest crevices of a poet's soul.

My muse lives in a fantasy
that reeks of clean sheets
on a secret bed
in a dark room where always there is water.

My muse enjoys the way of it
& gives no excuse
for wanting less stress
in complete undress.

No longer does she read poetry.
She will only read into her dreams
cut flowers on a nightstand
fragrant with the promise of romance.

I remove my clothes
& slide beneath cool sheets
next to her warm body.
She sleeps & dreams her fantasy.

I rise quietly & break quickly into a dance.

Chapter Fifty-Eight

I have other muses

Athletes, they are,
who incite me to write words.
I learned years ago
that words of love
most often fall on the deaf ears
of a page & hibernate.

For athletes with trim bodies,
small breasts,
firm hips, like the female
runners in ancient Greece, I write.
Their eyes see thru me,
such women,
even when my words flow
from me, like Old Seventy Creek,
onto the page.

My words are not their stream,
their beginning,
their underground source.
An athlete from Lesotho
once said to me:
*There are no lesbians
in my country.
Sex requires a penis.*
& I'm remembering Bill Clinton
on national TV as she speaks
so I asked her if she kisses women,
sleeps with them, & she says:
*yes,
& do things you'll never imagine*

Chapter Fifty-Nine

In case you read my poetry, Anna,

know this:
I have an understanding of how short
life is & I have forgiven you
too quickly
too often
for loving two of us
truly
deeply
madly.

I forgave you
when you kissed me slowly
then laughed uncontrollably
in the dark bedroom.

How quickly years pass...
How steadfast words hold their own
upon the page.

I finished setting your body free
from stone again this morning.

Chapter Sixty

Dear John

There was a time
when relationships ended
with a Dear John letter.

I received text messages
from you that broke
the news like this:

*When you find true love,
you have to leave certain things behind.*

*It's just I've liked this girl since I was a kid.
She never gave me the time of day
but she is coming around now and
when she does I want to be available.*

*I know it's not fair to you
that's why I'm letting you know (go).*

*I'll talk to you later.
I can't talk now.
So later, ok?*

*I'm really in love with her.
Anyway, I'm going now
and yes I have loved her forever.
That is true.*

Chapter Sixty-One

Akhmatova Taught Herself To Live Simply

& wisely,
to look at the sky and pray to God,
& to wander long before evening
to tire her superfluous worries.

While snow falls upon Old Seventy Creek
& brown leaves move like miniature flags,
their stems covered by an icy glaze,
I sit alone writing.

Nothing breaks the silence of my room.
Nothing!

Chapter Sixty-Two
Dominican Republic

Visiting the Old Town,
I saw the oldest fortress
ever built in the Americas,
built by the Spanish,
constructed in 1506,
an armory
designed to look like a church
& deceive enemy attackers.

I saw the oldest church
ever built in the Americas,
constructed in 1523,
& said to have housed
the bones of Christopher Columbus
before they were removed
to the Columbus Museum.

A woman, thin and light-skinned,
walking along the sidewalk,
looked so much like you
that a pain ran thru me
like water down Dunns River Falls
when we climbed it;
I was convinced you loved me, too.

On this island, alone,
& coping with being divorced
for one day,
I ask myself: *why does*
that thin and light-skinned woman
have to look like you
of all people?

Chapter Sixty-Three

Three women need to know

I should tell them how strong memory is.
I look into Old Seventy Creek
below the bridge & spring threatens
to explode daffodil, redbud, willow,
I see their faces as clear as a crescent moon
within a dark & cloudless sky.

I have loved them all,
but known only one
as my grandfather knew women
in a Biblical way
& I regret that,
for if I could touch the others
I would.

I would feel their naked bodies,
caress them with my lips,
embrace their charms
& stir the cold ashes of their neglected fires
until blue flames blaze.

If anything can carry me to them,
I will welcome it, the smell of mint along the
creek bank, sunlight captured in webs,
dew-drenched, across the preening pasture,
the dipping flight of a woodpecker,
but yearning cannot be so easily resolved.

Even tho they have stopped loving me,
I carry their secrets within.

Chapter Sixty-Four

A Guest, you are

since mid-January.
Most nights I hear you
come home.

It is
almost always midnight
when you unlock
the kitchen door.

A few minutes later,
I hear the freezer door
slammed shut
& the microwave

alarm five times,
but I do not hear you
tonight, tho I am awake
before your usual arrival hour.

I wake sometime after two AM.
I walk down the hall
past the bathroom
to your room.

The door is open,
three inches at most,
& the light is on.
You lie across the bed,

your legs, dangle,
pulled down by heavy, black boots.
It is not yet spring.
The room is cool & smells of booze.

I return to my room.
I get a blanket
& bring it to your room.
You have moved

but you are not awake.
Your short skirt
is twisted.
Your pink panties

have slipped to the right,
exposing the left half
of your parentheses.
An urge runs thru me.

I resist temptation; yet, write
the intensity of it into memory.
I cover you quickly
then quietly retire.

Come morning when you ask:
What happened last night?
I will tell you of the open door
& the blanket

but make no mention of punctuation,
nada of urges.

Chapter Sixty-Five
Even a mt. poet should be able to write something
about Maine.
Perhaps suggest that somebody's aunt
runs a restaurant
so far north that only hunters visit,
flown in by hydroplane.
Perhaps imagine it
as a place with few people
but many trees,
having at least one major mt. range that cuts
the horizon into a jagged line.
Baskets filled with chicken guts,
luring crabs, & crabs walking
across bare feet pinch flesh
which, if I am given to understand,
is a happening.
Such things about the land
might influence
which words go on the page
& how they sound.
& if the poet is to be believed, Maine
has beaches unlike those to be found
elsewhere along the east coast,
rocky stretches with high walls
for waves to lap against, & trees of boast
that rise out of winter snowdrifts.
Perhaps there is an inlet waterway (the poet sees
through other eyes than these)
that flows somewhere in Maine
& one expects its water to be cold even in
summer
but the water is warm through a mystery
the poet will not explain.

Chapter Sixty-Six

No Mystery to Explain

You came to see me
one afternoon, I remember,
& my eyes took you in
as tho you were a daffodil.

I will not write the feel
of poetry that began immediately when
sunlight filtered thru the window upon you,
words floating like dust upon the

beams of light. You asked to borrow the key
to my truck, for you had not eaten
since the night before. I handed them to you.
You turned to go then stood still.

Is there anything you want? You asked. The feel
came over me again & my answer
fell off my lips, house wren
like: *There is* I said. Patiently

waiting you expect me
to say something. You turned about again.
What? You asked. Again, I gave no answer.
You smiled; your boot heels

tap a rhythm on the hardwood floor,
all the way to the door.

Chapter Sixty-Seven

Poem in the Afternoon

I think about you when the rain begins.
I don't carry an umbrella.
Drops fall, sprinkles & little more.
I get damp as I walk.

I want you.
I want to write words across a page.
I want the words to be you.
It is possible.

I imagine rain falling
where you are. In my mind
you are a page
& I am crafting internal rhymes

all afternoon.

Chapter Sixty-Eight

Doubt

An Indian came to me
in his own dream
searching for his ancestral name
speaking Palouse
winging gracefully through the sky
like an eagle.

He did not ask me to soar with him—
did not imagine that I could fly.

Chapter Sixty-Nine

I Said

*come again with me
to Old Seventy Creek
& we will wade
& cross the field
to get to the rises
where if you remember
fragrant Honeysuckle
climbs out of the thicket*

*& when we disappear
in the shadows
we will leave our clothes
on the creek bank
where the Meadow Phlox
bloom reddish-purple
in sunlight
having found an opening*

*& we will play
like children
until Evening Primrose
opens near sunset
when I will rub
the lemon-scented
flowers that wilt
in sunshine*

across your lips.

Chapter Seventy

Into the Room Where Poetry Lies

The poet enters.
The room is bright.
The word awaits,
alluring as a naked woman
beneath a clean, white sheet.

The poet centers
his focus like a bird of night
upon the prey. The poet creates,
afterwards, when the emotions have run
their course on sensitive feet.

Chapter Seventy-One

Drawings from a Dream

I tried to have a dream about you
posing for me but I had intruders in the
dream. While you undressed, I heard
Modigliani telling Akhmatova
that he was writing poetry.

Modigliani kept telling Akhmatova
she was the subject of his words.
I will not hide my words from you he said.
*My words shall not be secret. I will trade them
with the world as tho they are statues.*

Modigliani kept telling Akhmatova
that she was his every fantasy
that he hoarded her as tho she were
heirloom jewelry, or silver, or gold.
The two of them talked mostly about poems.

& in my dream as you undressed, I heard
Modigliani tell Akhmatova:
*women with beautiful figures
who are worth modelling or drawing
always seem unshapely when clothed.*

This much I will say to you:
*Modigliani walked out of the dream
with Akhmatova under his umbrella.
They did not get to see how erotic you were
nor how shapely
& I tried so hard to draw masterfully.*

Chapter Seventy-Two

The End of a Novel

You stand in sunlight,
as beautiful as words across a page.
I desire you.

I approach you
& say
that tree is beautiful.

You look at the pink dogwood
in flowery bloom
then look at me with a

so what is your point
look
to which I respond:

*I appreciate beauty
in trees
& in women.*

You say nothing.
I get the feeling you think I see
the world through different eyes to yours.

I am reminded of Modigliani
who could see ugly people as beautiful
& stick by his opinion.

I see you as beautiful.
You think I only compare you
to some tree.

Chapter Seventy-Three

Writing a novel

Robert Penn Warren said
he gave up writing novels when
he realized they
took too much time
away from writing poetry.

Like Anna Akhmatova, the
Russian poetess whose rhyme
holds me sway,
I wait at night for words then
scribble notes within my head.

It is as tho I have no voice
except the words in my fingers.
If they come out as prose,
it is as tho I keep the sin some
call passion locked inside.

The sounds refuse to hide
& always overcome
the novel of my moment. A word goes
out from my sentence & lingers
like lips against a nipple. I rejoice.

Let me sin
that I might breathe again.

Chapter Seventy-Four
Picasso at Pere Lachaise cemetery

i.

The whole of Montmartre turned out Picasso said to Ortiz de Zarte after the funeral. *They say you found him.*

Montparnasse as well turned out. Yes, I found him Ortiz said *He was in a mess of a bed—empty bottles and half-opened cans of sardines dripping oil. Jeanne sat beside him. She never considered calling a doctor. I did at once...*

Too late, I hear to save him...

It was. He never came to after that. Such tragedy... I heard what you said about the policemen who lined the streets of the procession as we came to this place...

Do you see?
Now he is avenged. Picasso repeated.

Same prudes who closed down his show...

Picasso frowned. *& all they could say for themselves—their reason...*

With the nudes! They've got p-p-p-pubic hair! Ortiz laughed; Picasso frowned...

I'll leave you with Max Oritz said.

ii.

*You have to admit, My Beloved, Dedo was
extremely handsome* Max Jacob said to Picasso.

The women flocked to him Picasso said. *He was a
man who knew how to dress...*

*First time he saw you, he said you needed a
tailor or something along those lines to me. Anna
was his first love* Max said, speaking softly.

*His works are filled with her presence.
She brought out the poetry in his art* Picasso said.
After her, women came and went...

Until Beatrice Hastings Max agreed. *Will you ever
forgive me for showing up drunk at you lover's
funeral?*

*I should never do that, Max. Eva Göuel was dear
to me. What is worse, you tried to seduce
the driver of the hearse.*

*In the midst of friends, instructed by angels,
I was unaware of myself and I wrote...*

I enjoyed the poem you sent me Picasso said.

You recognized the lines from my poem:
To Mr. Modigliani to Prove I'm a Poet.

*If one cubist cannot recognize another cubist's
work, then both are dead already, Max.*

iii.

It is so good to see you again, my Fauvist friend Picasso said to Kees van Dongen.

You will be the most famous of us bohemians but Dedo will always be the best example of what I have heard you call...

Bad behavior romantically regarded as quintessentially artistic Picasso smiled.

*He missed you, as have I and Max and the rest of us from the **Bateau-Lavoir**, as Max dubbed that seedy Montmarte tenement where you lived* van Dongen said.

Dedo's excesses were such that I wearied of them and we drifted apart. Our circle of friends is getting smaller Picasso said.

Maybe we were nothing more than the circle of friends of Guillaume Apollinaire but the Great War delivered him that head wound, his death blow, so now we will be remembered as the circle of friends of Pablo Picasso...

We have shared things... You... I... Picasso nodded.

Women, opium, ambergris, and eroticism...

Picasso frowned, remembering Fernande Olivier before saying: *You and Dedo always cultivated a carefree bohemian image...*

Van Dongen replied: *Yes, I've always played. Painting is nothing but a game. A naked woman is the embodiment of all Art.*

Dedo's reputation will be dominated by his nudes Picasso mused.

You called me your Fauvist friend, but all of us truly are "les vauves"...

Yes we are wild beasts as men but not as artists Picasso said.

You know Dedo and I created such stirs with our nude exhibits...

His erotic female nudes... Your licentious nudes... Your lush colors... His subdued tones...

The essential thing is to elongate the women and especially to make them slim. After that it just remains to enlarge their jewels van Dongen said. *You cube them. Dedo knew how painting is the most beautiful of lies as do you and I.*

We were so poor when we came here, Dedo and I. You mentioned Apolline. Someday I will write poetry, too, like Dedo and Appolline. Today I will share my favorite lines of Appolline's as my memory recalls them:

(**Dead in whiteness and riches
Of snow and ripe fruits
Deep in the sky**

The sparrow hawks cry
Over the sprites with green **hair** *the dwarfs*
Who've never been loved
In the far tree-lines
the stags are groaning).

Your speaking of being so poor reminds me of what my Fauvist friend, Maurice de Vlanminck said to me van Drongen said. *I can quote him:*

I was poor but I knew that life is beautiful. And I had no other ambition than to discover with the help of new means those deep inner ties that linked me to the very soil.

iv.

I feel like the widow here Picasso said when Moise Kisling approached him. *I was thinking about you a few minutes ago.*

I hope you had one good thought Kisling said.

I thought about you volunteering for the French Foreign Legion. I thought how lucky you were to be seriously wounded and survive. And I thought how much the world would have lost if it had lost both Appolline and you...

The Battle of the Somme... July 1 until November 18... Neither side can claim victory... Such a waste of young lives... It seems like yesterday but it has been almost four years now. I suppose I could be called a winner. My wound earned me French citizenship.

Dedo painted you Picasso changed the subject from war to art.

In 1916, after I was wounded...

He did my portrait, too. I have several of his works. My favorite, I believe, is **Girl with Brown Hair.** *You must drop by and see it.*

Dedo was a close and caring friend. You must come by and see his portraits of me and the wife...

I will do that. If you will permit me to say something Picasso said...

Surely...

It will not be for your landscapes that you will be remembered Picasso said. *Like Dedo, your nudes will bring you fame.*

Do you remember the night Dedo, imbibed, raged through the studio and destroyed our paintings?

I remember Picasso said. *He destroyed all his early works soon after that.*

He knew the names of more beautiful paintings than anyone I ever met. His nudes capture the soul of the models. Where would art be without the female body?

On cave walls, perhaps, Picasso said, thinking about painting a mural someday. *Dedo's nudes are neither goddesses nor whores. They are naturalistic...*

Never passive Kisling interrupted.

Your nudes are realistic Picasso said. *That is the difference.*

v.

It was 1913 when you came to Paris Picasso said to Chaim Soutine.

Yes it was Soutine admitted. *I lived humbly in a circle of other Jewish émigré artists.*

Chagall, Lipchitz, and Kisling, Picasso said. *I remember. We were all hungry then going in the same direction but on different paths.*

I believe I developed my own style in 1918. Dedo was doing his best work the year before... Soutine explained.

Yes, he was. Inspired by the human figure... I count you as his closest friend and greatest admirer.

Thank you, Picasso. Always a pleasure to talk with you... Tell me something profound before I go.

Art is such a lie Picasso said.

vi.

If it isn't Constantin Brancusi Picasso said, *the world's foremost sculptor...*

If it isn't Picasso Brancusi said, *the world's foremost liar...*

Picasso grew silent.

I heard you talking with Soutine Brancusi laughed. *I do believe of all of us, you will be the best of the lot.*

You know, today, my favorite work of yours is Sleeping Muse...

Why is that?

It reminds me of Dedo's work...

His sculptures? Brancusi asked.

You made a sculptor out of him, no doubt, insisting he study African art. The masks did it. The elongated faces... Dedo's art will come to be recognized for his use of elongated figures and for his simple but monumental use of line.

What was your favorite sculpture of mine before?

Princess X Picasso said *as will it be tomorrow. Art should create a scandal now and then.*

vii.

Dedo and I grew apart Picasso said to Gino Severini.

We all took him in to whatever circle we belonged to at the time. We can be proud of that. I befriended him when friendship was all I had to offer Severini said. *Your fame is bringing you money. His work and mine never provided us enough to live on.*

I know what it was like to be dependent on the generosity of patrons Picasso said.

Vlanminck, Derain, and I will be waiting for you at the gate. We're going to the Cafe de la Rotonde. Come be bohemian with us again...

I will join you shortly Picasso said.

I see that Lipchitz, Léger and Foujita have joined them now Severini said.

Then let us leave our Dedo to his new circle of friends and go inquire about Jeanne first, shall we?

You haven't heard?

Heard what?

Jeanne Hébuterne leaped out of her parents' fifth story apartment and killed herself.

Chapter Seventy-Five

**Artsy, museum-going men
are happier, study says**

I sit here
inside the Speed Museum of Art
in Louisville, Kentucky,
drawn to Brancusi's *Mademoiselle Pogany I.*

I draw you from
memory as Modigliani
in the solitude of his room would have
drawn Anna.

I see Picasso's *Woman in the Studio.* I cannot get
inside Picasso's feelings. I shake my head.
In his work, Jacqueline, his last love, sits,
drawn in sharp profile.

I miss you in the company of such genius.

Chapter Seventy-Six

Upon hearing of Modigliani's death, Anna takes up her first published book, *Evening* and reads:

When you're drunk it's so much fun –
An early fall has strung
The elms with yellow flags.
We've strayed into the land of deceit
And we're repenting bitterly,
Why then are we smiling these
Strange and frozen smiles?
We wanted piercing anguish
Instead of placid happiness. . .
I won't abandon my comrade,
So dissolute and mild.

1911 (Paris)

The End

www.ingramcontent.com/pod-product-compliance
Lightning Source LLC
Chambersburg PA
CBHW060204050426
42446CB00013B/2981